G000071030

ELIZABETH KURANGWA

Be Ready No Retreat

RM PUBLISHERS
THE PUBLISHER OF CONFIDENCE

Contents

Foreword

Thank you for taking your time to read through my writing and making sense out everything I have written.

This is my 3rd book with your support. Be Ready-No Retreat is following John 14: 3 when Jesus promises His disciples that He will come back to take them to where He will be.

The Bible tells us that whosoever believes can have eternal Life. Jesus set the path for us, to follow as He called the twelve. He said once on the plough, there is no looking back. He chose for His disciples from hard working men, whose jobs required calculation and understanding times, they had determination in their variety of jobs. I then looked at a programme I like, Planet Earth, the Naturalists are so determined to follow and record every detail of the animals they are following to the end.

The animals are also determined to live and achieve their expected end of life plan, even if it means death.

Jesus was sent by the Father, and He sends us into the world to continue His work according to the Father's plan. He gives us a path to follow. Let the dead bury the dead.

It was then that the title of this book was just there so I started writing. Even where there is death, when you answer to His call there is no retreat. You follow Him to the end of your chosen path. You have been chosen to follow.

Once on the plough there is no looking back. Be READY -THERE IS NO RETREAT.

This is preparing for eternal life. It is an individual journey. It is a spiritual journey. Whosoever believes, Jesus said the Path is narrow.

Following my own life story of dreams, visions and trials, I have put a few things that made me remain encouraged to believe in all my circumstances. My dream walking on the narrow path sums it up well. As I followed the men on the narrow path, in every turn everything evil gave way. Jesus said, "Follow me."

He prayed to the Father. He gave us permission and authority to conquer.

He said the path is narrow but when He leads, when you follow His way, you will use the word as He did it as it is written, in confidence.

Faith+word, as it is written, directed to principalities in heavenly places, in Jesus' name means the battle is worn. The narrow path becomes a pleasure as the evil one falls like lightning when you say Jesus. The more you break powers and principalities, the more He leads. There is no reason to turn.

BE Ready! There is no retreat.

In the two books I have written, somewhere I had an unusual encounter with the Lord. But I can't say much. On 18/04/2020, I found myself in Heaven. I was given grace to understand and know what I saw without a guide or supporting voice.

My hearing mode was turned to zero. I heard nothing. I knew whatever I was allowed to see and I knew where I was going next, I also knew I was in the Court Yard of those that will be sealed, hundred and forty four thousand,[Revelation 7:4].

I saw GOD'S People as they are written in the Bible from Moses to the Sons of Zebedee. I knew the story of everyone I saw. Then it was time up, I wanted to make my prayer in the presence of all these Great God's People it had to be right.

I knelt down but did not know how to pray in front of these great people of God, so I asked the Lord Jesus to help me. From kneeling in heaven, I was now on planet Earth via Huntingdon England, woke up at 0230hrs in my bed in March England, nothing un usual happened. I was still me.

As a person I have not changed. I still laugh a lot. Am still working but towards the end. I still pray for lots of things that are in my heart. I have so much faith in God that what He did for others at the right time He will make everything plain for everyone to know He is God forever.

Pray without ceasing.

Let's pray for our enemies.

1

I DID NOT KNOW

I n my previous book, *Just As I Am,* a book about my dreams
and visions, I had no thought further than that the dreams
I was having encouraged me to pray. They helped me to
continue trusting that someone in that dream led me or when I
was falling, I called Jesus and someone said St Jude. But there
was thunder and lightning so it was powerful to trust Jesus. The
dreams and visions gave me confidence in my prayer life but I
had no understanding that these were verses in the Bible.

As I was growing up, I was not exposed to Christianity. We
never had a Bible; this was not influenced by my personal life; I
had no idea. This is who I am. I had dreams as long as I could
remember talking to my father about things that I should not
know but I knew them and I made sure my father understood
that, because whatever the dream was it was made clear to me.

They could have been visions but how could I know. When
I went to a secondary school, I loved Galatians 2:20 but it has
never been part of my dreams.

After and during the writing of *The Fathers Voice* I understood the Lord wants to communicate with us and had a few encounters with the Voice communication. It gave me the shivers and weakness in my body, but still I did not think much about these visions and dreams.

As I read the Bible, I found out that there is actually a verse that relates to my dream. I understood the verse as it was made clear in my dream only, I never knew they were scriptures. Sometimes when I mentioned my dream, I was told the scripture, but it's different when you read with a bit of understanding.

I will give an example of my song *There is a River in the Vision* I was walking and praying in tongues and singing most part of the night as a family member was not well. I came to this river and I saw the person washing in the river, by the morning I could now sing in English.

Indeed, it is a healing song. That is what I believed just that it's a healing song. Then when I read Revelation 21 John says there is a river and I knew that is the river I saw, and I knew it.

I walked by the river and actually the family member who washed in the river was healed. I stood by the river. Reading about the river John wrote about in the book of Revelation, changes to be just a song and reveals that even at our present day the Lord can still show us Hidden things of God's Kingdom without even our understanding until the time comes for it to be revealed.

Jesus sent the seventy to use His name to heal the sick, cast out demons and raise the dead. When the Seventy came back they said, "The spirits submit to us in your name." Jesus prayed to the Father and said, "I saw Satan fall like lightning."

I did not know that verse till January this year when I felt I should read the book of Mathew. Though in my prayer, after the dream, I believed it was powerful but without understanding. Now I understand that in Jesus' name when we pray Satan is defeated and falls like lightning, only in Jesus' name.

I have just given a few examples, just to say the Lord knew I had no knowledge of His Holy book and made me dramatize the scriptures so I don't forget.

It is like the Spirit was saying it as it is written. But without reading the Bible I would not have known such favour.

Still in my book *Just as I Am,* the encounter in the forest has made me stand against situations just because I was told in the dream that what I was afraid of was smaller than what I saw with my own eyes during the day as I herded my father's flock.

Still it gave me courage to say I will fear no evil but I still did not understand the Psalmist says in the Bible [though I walk in the shadow of Death I will fear no evil.]

I knew I was not afraid and I also knew that I couldn't stay in a forest. The fear came when the vision was replaying my encounter in the forest, seeing the little girl wearing a dress made of Gloria flour bags, seeing a tiny little stick to wave the grass out of my way, walking with my eyes fixed on the ground, and so close to the evil.

That made me shiver but on that day I had not even a thought of fear. This is fear no evil in action, I can't forget. As I look back I knew the gorge was too wide for me to cross or the Lord just stopped me to cross so I was not in the path of this whirlwind I was watching [Read *Just As I Am*].

I know that that day I was not meant to come home, I now understand I was meant to disappear forever and never to be found but the Man above was watching just like a chess player, he moved the right move and I am alive, just to say He is Alive forevermore.

If I had not seen the vision, I could not have known I was in imminent danger, it is like my Book of Life was opened for me to see what the Lord had done for me. In 2019, after someone read the book *Just As I Am*, they wanted to know how I could stand and even observe the colours of the monster that was passing in front of me, I just said surely there was no grain of fear, but I just stood there watching the evil pass in front of me.

Then after I finished my second book *The Fathers Voice*, I had a vision of what happened that day. It was like the little girl was standing there in a white wedding dress.

I could not see myself except this pure white-like dress had covered me completely. I understood what I could see but the enemy did not see me. When I wrote in the book, I said the Lord covered me but I did not know that He truly covered me completely.

I understand because the vision made it clear. That is why I feel no fear at all. When the Word says do not be afraid believe His action is so quick like a chess player, He makes a move to win, He is always the Winner.

I am just trying to explain that I did not know that the Lord was showing me or teaching me through these visions and dreams. They are actually what is written in His Holy book the Bible. It is true but all beyond my scope because, the Lord had mercy on me to take me and walk with me in the narrow path with no moon no sunlight, and when I read in the Bible I know how it looks like when there is no moon or sunshine because in my dream on the narrow path; that is how it was.

I did not know that. I now understand why even my father

wanted to see the things I saw they are supernatural and I did not know that is why I spoke openly, I had nothing to hide. The word of God says, "I know the substance that formed you, I knew you while you were in your mother's womb."

I never asked for any dreams or visions. I never prayed, it was just freely given. What can I say to my God for such a great favour? All I can do is write down whatever I feel the Spirit leading me. I have learnt a lot about seeing things that other people don't see, so I usually keep things to myself.

A messenger might not be able to explain deeper things, but Jesus the author and finisher of our faith is ready to communicate with all of us through the Holy Spirit. Also, to understand, I might not explain things deeper as I am going to relate to the Word of God and my journeys, He has shown me hidden things they are of the Spirit. Those led by the spirit of Truth will understand even better than I do. As usual, the messenger cannot speak for the Master. When I heard the voice saying "Write, why are you not writing?" I have that fear of keeping messages to myself which are meant for the body of Christ.

In all my books I try to make it clear that I have this gift so that maybe the message may be clear and not overshadowed by the unusual experiences that I right down. Looking at the dreams and songs that are verses, I think the Lord is showing me that the promises are still standing as they have been since the beginning.

The Lord answered my prayers in songs, and I have found that these songs are also some verses from the Bible so I believe the Lord is Just saying I have not changed my words are still valid as it is written.

When the voice said "Write it down" I thought what? My life

is empty, it was not about me. It was about His presence in our life no matter our circumstances that is why am writing. Just to let someone know that just like me they are loved.

No matter what people call you God sees the heart. Even as I started writing I did not even know one needs a title. Just as I Am somehow, I knew the title, I just wrote it without thinking. Still it was not about me for before I received the message that the book was on its way for checking, I saw in the sky the Lord's cloak at the back was written Just as I am. But I never say it because He enables people through the Holy spirit to understand it's about Him.

It is all about Him but I was thinking it can't be a book, my life is nothing. I did not know it was about Him. Harm not the Little children in action. I am still finding a lot of things I did not know that the Lord did and I thought it was one of those things that happen to me, as I always see things.

2

THE FATHER'S WILL

God so loved the world that He sent His only Son. To show us the way to eternal life, Jesus chose twelve disciples. He chose hard-working men, fishermen, field workers and a tax collector. These hard-working men were all acquainted with time and season.

They were also determined in their work to achieve certain goals according to time and season. They were acquainted with calculation and writing. Many of God's people starting from Moses were asked to write it down, so these were going to learn and write it down as we can still read what they wrote [Write it down]. With their knowledge they planned to achieve their intended goals.

When He called the Twelve, one wanted to go back to bury their loved one, but Jesus said let the dead bury the dead. Another just wanted to say goodbye to the family, but Jesus said once you are holding the plough you can't look back. So once He calls you and you say yes, There Is No Turning back. So, no matter how different our jobs are, Christ has a role for all workmen.

There is always a vacancy in His kingdom

Jesus of Nazareth taught His disciples scriptures and walked with them in synagogues. He read the scriptures. He gave them wisdom and was preparing them for when He was gone, they must continue His work to fulfill the Father's will.

Jesus tells His disciples how He must fulfill the scriptures as written by the prophets.In John chapter 17 Jesus prays to the Father, in verse 4 He says, "I have finished the work you sent me to do." Then He asks the Father to bless us all, whosoever believeth, will have life eternal. That is our destination. we must walk the narrow path to get to that place where we will be with Him forever, no sunset, no sunrise! Hoop hoop!

3

PREPARATION—BE READY

The Lord Jesus prepared His disciples for fieldwork on their own. They were given power for their mission. Power over unclean spirits, power to heal the sick and to cast out evil spirits and to raise the dead.

He told them of the perils that awaited them on their journey. He said, "I send you like sheep among wolves. Be wise as a serpent and calm as a dove. Beware of man, they will deliver you to courts." And then He reassures them, "Don't worry what to say, it will be given to you. My Father's Spirit will speak inside you."

Jesus gave them a warning, if they called the Master of the house Beelzebub how much more will they call His servants? Jesus told His disciples that the power is freely given and they must give freely.

Besides having faith in the Word of God, it's important to know that when He calls you for His fieldwork, He will give you power for whatever or wherever He sends you. In Ezekiel Chapter 8, God says to Ezekiel "Do not be afraid I have made your face strong against their faces, I have also made your foreheard stronger than theirs."

If you know the Word of God and you believe you will go. Because you become a new creation depending on what you are called to do. You become that peculiar person and you know if He sends you, He gives you power. Jesus on the cliff, when He was tempted, He defeated the devil by the written Word of God.

When you are afraid speak it as it is written, fear will run away from you. It will disappear instantly as if nothing happened. Fear will be replaced by peace. And then you remain as cool as a dove. As long as you use your faith and the spoken word with confidence.

But besides perils on the path to prepare for the everlasting Kingdom, there are warnings that are written. I will include this in the preparation for fieldwork as this warning was given to me in the form of a clear voice and given this scripture. Ezekiel 3:18-20.

Briefly the Lord says to Ezekiel, "If I send you to warn others and if you don't, and if this person dies in sin you will be held accountable."

I was given the chapter because when I was asked to write *Just As I Am* I thought it did not make sense. So I stopped writing. A voice asked "Why are you not writing?" Then I wrote but I had used my hand-writing so I could not do document, though I had a laptop, just the fear of technology so I just kept it.

But when I read that scripture I knew or found out what to do, it took more than a year the book siting in the drawers but I made a quick move after that scripture.

Find your calling He will cloth you with power. Do not judge yourself like I did. John 3:16 says that "Whosoever believeth in Him Shall not perish." There is always a way out when the

Lord sends you, it's only when you pay attention to His word that you find the open way to do His mission.

Even the prophets of old always said [JUST AS I AM]one way or another. When the Lord sends you its huge and fills you with fear but He is always there. I can tell you because I am the least person to be writing like this, technology is not my cup of tea but He enables me to do so.

He guides you, and guards you throughout the assignment, and makes the revision with you to check if you got it right. Just pay attention to the presence of His Holy Spirit, you are not alone.

Speaking about the spoken word, I can say this little dream it might help someone. I was under attack, something ugly was coming to me fast. I picked my Bible to shield myself but the thing did not stop. It seemed to have increased speed towards me even with my Bible as a shield. It seemed to have increased its velocity as if the Bible was making it come even faster. Then I called on Jesus, as someone under attack, I called so He could hear it was an urgent call. It was so loud so that the person next to me gave me the elbow to wake me up.

That was confidence in Jesus even in my dream. I called just once and it was gone. Then I continued my sleep, as cool as a dove. I always sleep with the Bible or Bibles but from that dream I learnt the Bible sitting there by my side without me speaking against evil is not effective against evil. Speak the word as it is written.

4

PARDON

I n many countries, at a certain time of the year, the head of
the government pardons one convict. They are released
and their case is closed [deleted]. Even in the Days of our
Lord Jesus of Nazareth, there was a time where one prisoner
was to be pardoned.

Though they had seen miracles which they knew were
recorded in the scriptures, they could not decide for Jesus to
be pardoned. The Lord had made a decision, before the Father
that He will be led to the slaughter like a sheep. His blood would
be for the atonement of our sins. All our sins will be pardoned
never to be remembered.

So, they could not call His name for pardon though they knew
He changed water into wine, that He made the blind to see and
raised Lazarus from the dead. The Lord was determined to be
treated as the lowest of the low just because [God so loved the
world]. He wanted to do it so we can be called the children of
God. So we can be with Him always at the appointed time.

I have not met anyone who has received a Presidential Pardon
to ask how it feels. When they know they have committed a

crime suddenly the crime is forgotten, that is what was done for us. A pardon for all our sins. After they are released the convicts are on their own. We are so loved that Jesus promised that once He is gone, He would send a comforter who will be with us always. So even if you are alone you know there is the Holy Spirit to help you and keep you encouraged that Jesus loves us, that just as He was with His disciples, through the Holy Spirit He cares.

In Romans 8, Paul tells us that we received the spirit of adoption and it cries for us [our Father]. Jesus did not get the pardon so we can be called the children of God and indeed we are. As it is written.

In Colossians 1: 13-15, it states that He delivered us from the power of darkness and conveyed us into the kingdom of Heaven.

Ephesians 4:30 warns us not to Grieve the Holy Spirit.

In Exodus 23:20-23, God told Moses He is sending an Angel before him. In verse 21, the Lord said "Beware of Him, do not provoke him. He will not pardon your Transgression, my name is in Him." If you obey His voice, God will fight your enemies.

Our shield against grieving the comforter is to keep the Laws of our God and hear the Holy Spirit as He is there to keep us safe until our Lord Jesus Christ comes to take us so we can be with Him always. He paid for our Pardon from all our sins. Let us rejoice like a prisoner who has been set free.

Jesus paid the debt for all our sins. If we believe, we are set free from the bondage of sin by His blood that was shed on the cross. There was no retreat.

5

PASSING THROUGH JERUSALEM

A s the time was near for Jesus of Nazareth to fulfill what was written about Him by the prophets, He took some of His disciples to go and pray in the Mount of Transfiguration. He took John, Peter and James. As Jesus prayed on the Mountain the disciples saw Elijah and Moses with Jesus. It was time for Jesus to pass through Jerusalem to suffer all tribulation and humiliation, they came to strengthen Him.

It was time to prepare for passover. Jesus was sorrowful knowing the time was near for Him to suffer, and also to leave His disciples alone. He told His disciples what He will go through. Jesus had taught them all He could at the time, soon they would be on their own.

Now their Rabbi, their Master, will be led to the slaughter like a lamb for the sacrifice of all our sins. Though Jesus told them He will be taken by the rulers of that kingdom, they did not know the shame that was awaiting Him in Jerusalem. Jesus knew they would be scattered and that Peter would deny Him.

He had come to do the Father's will. "For God so loved the

world and gave His Son." This was the Father's will, it was His willingness to be led like a sheep ready to be slaughtered.

He needed to pray to the Father, He took His disciples to Gethsemane and left them as he went further to pray. He prayed to the father to let the cup pass. He made this prayer three times. Every time He came back to His disciples, they were asleep. They did not know the shame that would befall their Master being spat at, beaten and pushed although He was there before the world was created, He was the word of God.

He was determined to get over it with strength from His Father and all the prophets in Heaven gave Him support. As there was none who was found who could take His Place, He carried the cross being pushed and beaten, yet He uttered no word. He was doing the Father's will. He carried the shame through Jerusalem to the cross. Being human it would be devastating for the disciples to see their Master, their teacher, being humiliated. I think being scattered was a shield from the pain they would feel for their Master. The Lord always makes a way for His own.

6

PLANET EARTH

I t is a great relief to watch *Planet Earth,* the show. I switch on the screen with great expectation. It is a break from other programs that really don't seem interesting.

We are so grateful to the naturalists who give up everything and take us to the mountains, rivers, forests and to some dangerous places on earth just to show us a life cycle of a small creature which we may never heard of. But we still watch and learn.

It's their determination and resolve that make me watch the program to the end, the presenters never retreat. They show big lions, how they live, their clan, how they survive and that the are territorial.

It takes them as long as it takes to finish their task. Hey, we are grateful. They show us how little fish survive; we learn a hard-working life of an ant until death. They also show us the wars between same species of animal or creatures, they fight for leadership, for food and others fight to be the father of the clan.

The male lion cub knows someday he will have to fight with

his father so he can be the head of the clan. They cannot change, it's in their nature but when the time comes, they will fight even if it means they become an outcast or die during the fight. There is no retreat.

I love the little fish which grow and know when it's time to lay eggs. They must travel a perilous journey against currents of the seas, sharks and oceans just to get to that estuary to lay eggs and then die, like the previous fish of their type before them. If the fish survive, they will keep their fish kingdom alive, once accomplished they die. There is no retreat, it is determined to reach its expected end.

Just like animals and all creatures that fight for different reasons, we also as long as human history, have had wars for different things. We differ from animals because God created man above them all. And God so loved the World that He gave His Son to be made a sacrifice for all our sins if we believe so that we can have eternal life.

In John 14:3, Jesus said to His disciple "I go to prepare a place for you and I will come back to take you so that where I am there you may be also." This is a different kind of war, it is a spiritual warfare. This is about faith.

The oxford dictionary says, faith is a strong belief or complete confidence in your chosen path. So, to fight in this war you must believe Christ is the Son of God. In the book of Hebrews 11:6, it says "You cannot please God without faith."

The Apostle Paul puts it clearly, we do not fight against blood and flesh but against powers and principalities in heavenly places.

As in Daniel's prayer, God sent the Angel to fight the principalities of the King of Persia for Daniel to get the answer. This tells us that there are principalities that affect individuals, communities and nations as Daniel was praying for a nation that had moved away from their God.

That is where our war zone is. In Heavenly places. While the Lord prepares a place for us, we need to know there are perils in that path Mathew 7:14 tells us "It's a narrow path and narrow gate that leads to life." This reminds me of my dream about The Narrow Path. When I said the narrow path, it was not because of this scripture above [I did not know the scripture].

The path I walked was very narrow with all fierce animals roaming about, coming to cross right in front of me but as I approached, they gave way as I was focused to the man who was walking before me. He was leading the way. [I did not know my Lord.]

I was not afraid of all the beasts roaming about. The Lord made me walk the narrow path and I saw evil giving way and He was leading. I cannot forget because I did not just see it but I walked on the narrow path. As He said to His disciples, Do Not Be afraid, I was not afraid as I walked with all those fierce creatures roaming around.

There was no sunlight or moonlight but still there was some light not bright [May be light as at dawn]. Just like the Naturalist and animals and creatures, let's find our destination by faith and determination. No Retreat. So that when the time is up for us, we can be sure our Lord will be our light forever. Be ready!

7

IT IS FINISHED

Jesus came to show us the way to prepare for eternal life. He chose Twelve workmen to be the ones to carry on what He had started. His chosen were hardworking and diligent men. He taught them in parables and took them to the Synagogue so they could continue when He was gone.

He taught them how to pray and told them it's going to be hard but He would send the Comforter. He gave all knowledge and wisdom they needed. When He had gone through all the shame in Jerusalem, when that cup He had asked the Father to do His will was accomplished, indeed the shame was finished on the cross.

When He rose, He took His rightful place at the right hand of the Father. To Reign for evermore. His chosen workmen were given Authority according to John Chapter 17 and they travelled to preach the Gospel of Christ despite persecution. They believed the words of their Master.

They passed the words of the Master to everyone who believed, the same Authority belongs to every believer. That He will come back to take us so that where He is, we may be there also.

They preached the Gospel as we also know it today. We believe He is coming back shining like the sun to present all those that believe to the Father, the King of Kings, the Ancient of Days. Workmen are you Ready to follow Him?

He says Follow me, there is no retreat if you do. But the road has perils like little fish facing opposing currents and big sharks to reach their destination. The little fish have to lay the eggs for the Fish kingdom to keep expanding. He says I will be there with you. Always Be ready He is coming to take His own to the Mansion prepared for each one of us who believe.

8

FAITH

The Bible tells us God is Spirit, those that worship Him must worship Him in Sprit and in truth. Hebrews 11:6 says, "Without faith we cannot please God."

The Oxford dictionary says, faith is strong belief and a person has confidence in their belief. This explanation makes you understand that to have that belief you need to know your subject and how it works so you can have confidence. As Christians we believe in God, we believe He loved us, we believe He sent His son and that Jesus will come again.

Jesus said with little Faith as a mustered seed we can move mountains. As the Oxford dictionary says there is no proof it is difficult to discuss or teach it as you cannot measure faith.

What we know is that if we want to connect to God, we need faith. I am not a theologian but I will try to say it the way I feel it helped me keep my faith in God. All the knowledge we need to know so we can have confidence in our faith is the word of God. The Apostle Paul in Hebrews 11 explains and lists biblical figures who went through situations by faith. It is better to give examples as you cannot prove faith, but the results of faith can be said as testimonies to encourage others.

We connect to God by faith. The word of God makes us understand what we believe in and gives us that confidence we need when our faith is shaken. It is like the umbilical cord connected to the mother and nutrients feed baby and make it grow. When you read the Word of God, it's like nutrients, you gain confidence and grow in your faith and confidence.

Psalms 110:10 says, "The fear of the Lord is the beginning of wisdom and understanding to those that keep his commandments." This is the benefit of faith connected to the word of God you learn His promises, His laws and gain confidence in your faith. King David says, "Thy word will I keep in my heart so that I cannot sin against thee." The word becomes your weapon that protects you against doing what is wrong before God even though others think it is right.

Jesus said "it is written" because He read the scriptures. When you are under attack you use the word by your faith. I like the Oxford definition that faith is complete confidence. Without the Word, your faith is shaken and can be affected by other philosophies. It may also lead to abuse by false doctrines because you did not get the correct growth from the Word of God.

The Oxford dictionary says wisdom is accumulation of knowledge, just like nutrients from the umbilical cord makes the baby grow and is delivered when it matures, studying the word will strengthen your faith in God.

You know God's laws and keep them according to His instruction then you gain wisdom and become obedient to His will. You don't make an effort for anything, your faith is grounded then you get the fruits of obedience and endurance when things are not right.

You always have hope so it keeps your mental state stable because you hope for better. When you are in doubt you go to the word of God, you know the Spirit leads you and you wait in faith for His guidance. Then your faith will produce fruits as the Lord sends you like the twelve disciples. We are to go to the utter most parts of the world to find lost souls and bring them into His fold. The fact that there are so many Churches means people are looking or seeking for something. Check it out, you might be the one the Lord is sending.

In my example, I think if I had not moved to the Isle of Man, I would not have had this encounter with the Lord, sometimes places become a muddy road and we stick to it when the Lord actually wants to meet with us somewhere else. I had faith in God that every place I went to He would take care of me.

I was not bothered by interviews. I always said if I go for an interview, I market myself. I usually got the jobs with no problem. I was not afraid to work with new people because I was always confident, they are God's people and I loved everybody wherever I went. So, moving was not a problem for me. But I did not know that till now that the Lord had plans for each place I went.

The Apostle Paul in Ephesians says faith is a gift from God, so it is a strong connection to God so you can hear His whisper even if there is no voice. My faith in God kept me confident that in this new city, new job, new workmates I will have no problem and indeed the Lord was my refuge. I now understand I did not just move, the Lord had plans for each and every place I went to. He is the Prince of Peace even if it is just to make people laugh, if the Lord sends you, there is a reason.

But I did not know till I wrote the Book the *My Father's Voice* that the Lord told me about my work. I never thought my job had anything to do with God till that day. Still I can't talk about it. I still shiver thinking about it. All I know is that I needed to pray for protection at work, but the Lord needs us as sanctuaries for His work to bring peace to whosoever the Lord wishes to. Be ready to go.

With this faith and wisdom developed from little faith, I was encouraged to grow by the word of God, and other people's testimonies. Even those who were before us had to pass through perils like little fish so as to accomplish their set goals. The Bible becomes a safe house where you learn how to go along this narrow path the Lord tells us about.

Then you are ready for your journey in Christ. His advice, be wise as a serpent and calm as a dove, will become real. When you are obedient you don't feel or struggle, fighting like a serpent when you are obedient the spirit moves and guides you.

Because the Bible tells us we do not fight with flesh and blood but spirits in heavenly places. When you get the power from the Lord it is like light so wherever you go the spirits of darkness will see the light. If you are obedient you will respond by prayer and the spirit of darkness will flee and peace will come then you become calm as a dove.

You cannot do it on your own without your faith in God and the presence of the Holy Spirit and the written word. Psalms 27:9 says, "For with you is the fountain of life, in your light we see light." The light which is lighter than light hovers over you if you believe you cannot see it but by faith you know and believe. By faith you are connected to God, God is love, you cannot hate.

Because His word is on your neck Like David says it, [so that I cannot sin against you] I feel though I had faith in God, reading

His word has strengthened me in many ways. Though I did not know that the songs I received in my spirit were verses or they were the word of God, it was wonderful for God to answer my prayers in songs.

Now I can relate to the songs and dreams to the word of God and its more meaningful to me. I pray with confidence if things are not right for me, I don't panic because I know He is there in the middle of it all. Because He answered me in songs its real when I see its actually written, I believe. I don't get stressed by anything though people get stressed for me it's their business.

Faith and His word have made me understand that I can wish for so many things but if I can't make it God has a reason. It's His word that you believe and use it in your request to our Father in Heaven. You always know He answered that time and say to yourself I am just human; He is God He knows my needs and continue to worship Him.

I feel faith and the word of God are a good equation to give you Wisdom, which gives us wisdom to walk in the Spiritual realm to connect to God. Then we can be ready to walk among wolves knowing we have the sword of the spirit. Knowing His light is over us by faith. Because we know we were given power to overcome, the wolves will give way just as I saw it in my walk on the narrow path. They gave way. Jesus is real.

Talking about light 0n 09. 05. 2019 I had a dream. There was light in the sky. Like different rectangle bulbs of different sizes in the sky. In April this year, I went to a hospital and the lights looked so bright as in my dream. So, I phoned my friend to tell her about my dream and as if the lights I saw were similar to the light in my dream. Then she gave me this verse above.

I really want to say in my dream the light was lighter than light that is all I can say. There were many people going the same direction under this white light. A Voice spoke, "I can even hear your footsteps."

If he sends you, He puts you under His light. I can now understand all negative thoughts about me. I was always under His light yet I did not know it but now I get it.

Those who walk in the Lord will know the truth because the same light illuminates their Path. I am hoping to encourage someone to know that, whatever you desire to do for the Lord, He will never leave you alone. He will cover you like a Baby Kangaroo, completely protected in its mummy's poach always. Always keep your faith in God. He will never leave you alone, that is His Promise He does not retreat, He does not change.

9

PRAY WITHOUT CEASING

As we are all human, we do not know how we ought to pray. Jesus gave us a guideline on how to pray. It is a complete prayer as it touches Heaven and earth, our being and our sinfulness. Jesus promised to help us pray by sending us the Holy Spirit. Because each one of us are called to do different things. I think we cannot say there is a better way to pray. I think we can discuss the points that help us to connect to the Holy Spirit. We can also give testimonies to encourage one another to come before God with our requests.

We know if you have faith in God it's the only way to please God and when you study His word you know how He wants you to be. The word of God also tells us about our character, so that we can stand before God in prayer with confidence. You get wisdom from His word and knowledge and understanding.

As you read His word some verses get into your spirit more than others, you go over them even if you don't know why they are underlined in your spirit. The more you read the more you feel His presence in the words because you keep your faith as you read.

As you come to some verses, they become personalized such as, I will put my Laws in their mind and I will write them on their Hearts. By faith you believe as you pray you speak with God's laws inside you.

The Oxford Dictionary says wisdom is accumulation of knowledge. You now have knowledge and you fear to break God's laws. They are written in your heart, then you become obedient to God, you have trust and hope in your God. You persevere to keep the faith even when things are not right you continue your faith in God knowing the Holy Spirit is always ther You pray with understanding and you allow the Holy Spirit to take over.

When you allow the word of God and the Holy Spirit to flow you have a scripture for every situation if you know His word. You speak the word as it is written, keep the hope also listen to the Holy Spirit.

Sometimes we should pause to listen to the Holy Spirit. You might get a scripture for you to read or some guidance or even acknowledgement of your prayer. The Lord said we are not Listening to His voice. His promise asks and I will answer, and He says Try me.

The Bible in Romans 12:16 reminds us not to lean on our own understanding. When we think we have now got wisdom and disconnect from our faith in God, we lose that cord like the connection with the mother's placenta. Our faith is weak and we speak our knowledge without faith it does not bear fruits.

That is where our Lord will deny us. The presence of the Holy Spirit is God's gift. Some have gifts to lay hands and you receive the Holy Spirit. Just to encourage someone, sometimes even when you pray on your own you may speak in tongues. It happened to me. I was afraid because I did not know, but as you pray alone it's between you and the Holy Spirit.

I was on my own when I started, I did not know anything about the Holy Spirit so I prayed and the groaning started, I stopped praying. So, I could not pray among others in case they said it was Beelzebab. But when I read a book about intercession, I did not groan only but I spoke in tongues for the first time I could not stop. But still I did not know anything about speaking in tongues.

When you speak in tongues, they say it's a sign of the presence of His Holy Spirit. Then your Faith and hope in God leads you to pray without ceasing as in Thessalonians 5:17, Pray always.

Speaking in tongues is communication between God and us in Heavenly mysteries. Also, there is a lot we can hear and learn if we connect and allow the Holy Spirit to dwell and lead us into prayerfulness. It's not just a sign, you can get guidance as you pray. You can get the answer as you pray. We are to pray and take time to listen, meaning just rest your mind and spirit before God.

I have songs that come after praying and singing in tongues. I have poems that come after praying in tongues. Sometimes I get verbal prophesy after I have prayed in tongues. Pray in tongues is a conversation between heaven and earth with expectations.

The Holy Spirit is our comforter besides knowing He is there, we can get reassurance in our spiritual need if we allow ourselves time to listen. He will move us up to more of God's gifts.

Sometimes I have prayed in tongues for someone and later they tell me they were praying in the same tongues though I did not lay hands on them. The spirit works in mysterious ways, so we need that faith in God always to know it's the Lord.

God is Spirit, the Holy spirit is always around us. Some

tongues are for special situations and there are specific to the person to unlock a specific situation as the Spirit leads. I think that is why some people can impart tongues so that the individual can unlock closed doors on their own.

There is more in speaking in tongues besides being a sign, our Lord was a teacher. He left His Holy Spirit to teach us as we pray.

You can always find scriptures that seem to say something to you. Keep reading and you will find something personal from the word of God. When I read Daniel Chapter 9, his prayer has similarity to the Lord's prayer.

-Daniel started by praising the Lord

-He speaks about forgiveness

-verse 17, hear our prayers for our Lord's sake

-we present our prayers because of your mercies

-do not delay for your own sake

It helped me to know that the Lord's prayer is a complete prayer touching heaven and earth.

Praising the Lord and forgiveness are highlighted in Daniel's prayer. It helps me to focus on the Lord before I ask anything in prayer.

Somehow for many years, I was drawn to John Chapter 17, though I read it regularly still I did not get it. I even bought different Bibles to find if it is the same.

But one day I just read it as if it's very new, I was understanding it as if the Lord was telling me what He told His disciples. It was as if He was talking to me and I believed. I understood that Authority was given to me also. I have never stopped since that day to understand that I have the authority just as the twelve were given. I have confidence in that.

Let's take that garment of prayer and pray always because the one we Worship does not Slumber. This is the word adding fire to your little faith and then when you pray you don't think or write about it, the word and Spirit lives inside you, no struggle to pray. Especially when it comes to being glorified, it is powerful.

Being Glorified by His glory is an amazing feeling, you pray knowing that His light which is briggter than light is over you, you are not afraid of any situations. His glory is all we need.

Sometimes we can pray being very emotional due to our situation but if you rely on His word, emotion is not what moves mountains, it's the Faith. Sometimes what we are asking for is what the Lord is holding back for a reason.

The Holy Spirit will make us feel peaceful if we pay attention. Because I moved a lot, I went to different Churches, I did not get attached to church activities or to Pastors. When I saw the word Long-suffering, I thought that was me, so I prayed a lot on my own. With a lot of emotion and crying. I prayed aloud, I never stopped the tongues if they came, I let them flow.

I have got the reward of songs and poems afterwards, because I pray independently. I don't get stopped by programs; I just pray. I have been told by different people that I pray while I am asleep, really loud as if I am awake. By His grace I pray even if I am asleep, that is while we sleep, He does not slumber the Spirit in us continually pleading for us like little children, we are before our God.

I think that is praying without ceasing. The Lord fights our wars while we sleep. He will lead us by the green Pastures someday. Pray without ceasing. Now after reading through the Bible since 2015, I use my Faith and the word of God but I am less emotional as I use His promises. And hope He will answer my prayers, as God's promises are from everlasting to everlasting.

And God does not repent, it helps me to keep grounded in His promises. But sometimes it hurts, and you think of the Lord in Gethsemane, alone because those He took with Him fell asleep. You feel you are in a desolate, old rugged field; you cry a lot. Then the word of God comes [I am your Lord, I am your God I know your needs and I know your ways]. You feel peaceful the word of God will always comfort you in whatever situation but continue to pray without ceasing.

I say Gethsemane because when it was hard, our Lord went to Gethsemane to have a conversation with the Father. I go to my bathroom to pour my heart before my God. When your heart, your soul and spirit is hurting, you are like in a wilderness, with no one there all on your own, find the field of your choice talk to the Lord like what our Lord did in Gethsemane.

But pray always. The Apostle Paul says though I pray in tongues of man and Angels, without Love I am nothing. He says pray always in psalms and hymns, worshipping God. It is important to have love if you want to be a workman for Christ as He is yearning for those prodigals to be brought home without love for the lost it is difficult to bring them home to Christ Jesus of Nazareth.

When King David fasted for his son, the son died. David started eating and drinking because he knew God had done His will. God had made a decision and he ate and drank, because He knew his God. He had faith in God and trusted Him in every situation. He knew He was His Lord and God. Even when we pray and don't get what we asked for God has heard. He has good plans for us. Elijah prayed for the rain to come. He kept on sending a boy to check in the sky if the clouds were showing,

he did not stop praying.
Pray without ceasing.

10

ROAD TO DAMASCUS

When Jesus had gone to be at the right hand of the Father, He chose one more workman besides the twelve He had chosen.

This man was hardworking, determined and highly educated in the law of the country. He understood what a citizen should do to keep the country safe. Saul of Tarsus did not hesitate to go and get permission to persecute Jesus Christ's followers. He wanted it to be known that he was part of the Christian tormentors as he was holding Steven's clothes as he was being stoned.

He was part of it. He made his way to Damascus. But the Lord saw a hardworking man, committed to his job. He stopped him in the middle of the road. Like Jesus of Nazareth always does Suddenly! The Lord called him once and Saul knew it was the Lord. In Acts Chapter 9 we read the story of Paul. Paul was becoming a new man in Christ Jesus, the zeal he had to persecute the Lord turned it for His Glory. The Apostle Paul had worldly wisdom which was turned into God's wisdom.

Jesus read the scriptures to connect us to what the prophets foretold. The Apostle Paul made us understand that we can also have faith like Abraham because he was a person like us. He made us aware that Elijah was a person like us but he prayed to call down fire, he prayed for it to stop raining for a certain period and prayed for it to rain. In other words, we can also do it. The question is why can't we do it?

He clarifies the way to fight spiritual warfare by looking at a Roman Soldier going to war and thinks if we could do that for our Lord we can be like these soldiers. If the soldier lost one of his armor, he is not safe to go to war. Therefore, even us Christians if we don't know His word, we lose that full armor then we are not fit for His war. If you put on the full amour of God use it with confidence you will not be moved.

Paul is trained in the Law and his knowledge gives him wisdom to write letters to many explaining how God wants us to live. He connected his knowledge to produce wisdom to simplify difficult laws to make them understandable. He was a chosen vessel and he never changed. He imparted his knowledge to those around him and even us today we read his powerful messages.

They were not his alone. He was connected to the Lord by faith. The Lord made him write down so we can also meet Him on our way to Damascus and turn our lives around. Maybe we can also reach where the Apostle Paul says, [I have fought a good fight, I have finished the race and I have kept the Faith] Timothy 4:7.

It is clear that he was following the guidelines of the assignments he was given and knew he had finished his assignments.

He was ready now there was no turning back, like the little fish, he had reached the estuary and laid his eggs which is all the words and letters he wrote to advance the work of our Lord

35

Jesus, who was sent to us by the Father. The apostle was ready
for the End.

11

A WALK IN THE COURTYARD

I had done a night shift on the 17th of April 2020 and in the morning after work I felt unusually tired and did some house work so I could settle without worrying about things I wanted to do.

I settled in bed at midday. By 10 pm I was awake, sat a little and went back to sleep.

I have had visions and dreams, but this was different. I think that is what they call an out of the body experience. I don't even know what a trance is like. I did not feel or see anything that indicated I had died. All I know is that I was in Heaven.

I was in the courtyard as it is written in the book of Revelation for the 144 thousand.

There were people walking about. I was at the edge of the courtyard, it was like the people were on the east of the courtyard and I was on the west side so I could see them all on one side. There was a choir but I did not hear the singing, it was very quiet. There was no moonlight or sunlight. There was a giant lion which was lighter than the surrounding, though it seemed to be at the age of the courtyard it was above the courtyard, everyone could see, it looked like a lion in the form of light.

I knew that in heaven the roads are paved in gold so I looked down but as I looked down, I saw nothing though we were all walking in the courtyard. Still I knew I was in Heaven.

As I was walking, I was passing the Prophets as written in the Bible and I knew them, I knew their stories. I can list those I remember clearly. Elijah, Ezekiel, Naomi and Ruth, the Sons of Zebedee, the Apostle Paul, John the Baptist, Daniel, Aaron and Moses. I did not walk among them it was side by side as I was passing them.

I can say, to make it clearer, I was walking like north to south as I passed the Prophets one by one, then I turned eastwards, I knew I was going where King David was. As I walked, I knew he was anointed by God and the glory around him would be too much for me so I turned back. I also knew that as I walked in the courtyard someone was walking behind me but I never looked to see who was behind me.

It did not bother me; I did not think about it, I just knew someone was behind me. I came where I was passing the prophets now on the same side but am going northwards like going where I had started. At my back but more on my right I could see John the Baptist, I wanted to turn back and ask him about his head I could not turn but I really wanted to talk to him. I could see him without turning but only the bottom half he was shielded from his chest upwards. I did not see his heard or face. Of the living prophets, I saw Pastor Chris of the Christ Embassy. He was kneeling down praying in heaven in his white suit. I am not a member of his congregation. I just saw Him in Heaven.

As I was passing these prophets, I said I should pray while I am among these prophets of God. It was as if I knew I have to go somewhere but I wanted to make my prayer in the Presence of these amazing people of God gathered together. So, I knelt down and I still knew I was kneeling down in heaven.

As I was kneeling down, I wanted to say the right words in front of God's Prophets. That was very important to me to say the right prayer as I knew they are great man of God. Then I was thinking who could give me the right words to pray. I could not remember anyone who could help me with the correct words. I felt blank. Then I started to pray asking Jesus to help me to find someone who can give me the right words to pray. I had no thought process, I had no idea what I wanted to pray for, I so much wanted to make my prayer in the presence of these God's people. I did not hear any answer or voice from heaven. I only asked Jesus to help me find someone but I can't remember anything after my prayer for help. It was all quiet. As I was still kneeling down in heaven, I then found myself standing in a Church in Huntingdon; in the church I found Pastor reading from the Bible and I knew he was reading a scripture to guide the members of the Church about something. Then I woke up amd the time was 0230 am on 18 04 2020. I had started writing this book so all was written before this journey as I started writing on 05 04 2020.

In case what I wrote does not correspond with this. I wrote about the Apostle Paul on the twelfth of April.

I managed to get Pastor Huntingdon and I told Him my journey. He simply said I have three verses for you. He gave me three verses to read so I could make my prayer. It is Awesome and just as I am, I still feel that is what all ordinary people like me feel like when the unusual and unimaginable heavenly secrets are revealed. I still can't pray about the journey its huge for me.

Of my dream about Pastor looking for a scripture to correct a situation, His own words [I am shocked because that is what I did.] I felt the Lord wanted to confirm that everything I saw on my journey in the courtyard was real. My connection to Pastor Huntingdon; this is just to add Pastor Huntingdon allowed me for the past year to use his pulpit to talk to his congregation without reservation.

I have preached a few times in his Church. Now it is recorded in heaven because the Lord knew him. I know so because while I was kneeling down in Heaven the Lord sent me straight to him, and I saw him doing what he said he did. Pastor Huntingdon gave me the scriptures just like that straight and quick.

When I woke up, I did not feel anything like others say you can see your body no. Even when I was in heaven, nothing came to me about death. I felt overwhelmed by this for days. I could not think about writing this book I was blank.

But looking back and thinking about all the things I was crying to God about; none of them came into my mind, it was all about Heaven. I was not thinking about anything here on earth. I did not remember anything about my life on earth, it was not there. Even as I knelt down in heaven, I had no words to say though I wanted to pray. I wish I could shout about loving one another while we still live cause when we die, we will not remember.

It was going to be a great opportunity to say all my problems in heaven in the courtyard but all earthly things were no longer in me. I did not remember them except that I was in heaven. The desire to speak to John the Baptist was so strong, I know I wanted to ask about his head but I have no idea what my question was going to be. It was a strong feeling but without the words. I think the person behind me had to give me a push to continue as I think my time was limited.

The Lord knows that some people are a bit mad. He loves us Just as we are and He has a good sense of humor sometimes. I am thinking of the Preacher when He says all is vanity, because I really have something I am praying for, but when I was in heaven I did not remember anything or anyone, meaning everything had disappeared from me. I think that is why the preacher said all is vanity.

12

REWIND

I had been praying for a few months looking at the Prophet Ezekiel Chapter 37: 11-15 before the walk in the courtyard. I understood that the dry bones are everything of ours that we hoped for but did not materialize. I have a well which had no water. And I had hoped to retire and use the well to make a living so if the water is not there those are dry bones.

So, I prayed for water as I have no water what could I do? I could not afford to dig another well. The only thing was to pray, using the words according to Ezekiel and with confidence. I put my case before the Righteous Judge [There is water now in my well]. Truly my hope was lost but in God is hope.

The Lord spoke to Ezekiel, that He will open up the graves and take the people to their land. I started to prophesy to situations in my life, things that I hoped for but did not come to pass. I believed because it is His word and He does not change.

He is just as He was in the days of all the prophets. So, when I saw the prophets, I knew them very well but no message was given to me. My own feeling is that, as the Apostle Paul said about Abraham and Elijah the Lord showed me ALL the Lord's prophets. They were not great people in the things of the World but in God's Kingdom. The Lord is ready to lead us to war just like He did with the prophets of old. He is the word of God; He is the beginning and the end. They all thought they could not be the one to be sent, it is very difficult to say but on the other hand the fear of the Lord makes you strong.

Knowing He is there with you and the Holy spirit, who is a great prophet who lives in us will know the truth for those who seek to know. The Holy Spirit always confirms that which is from the Lord.

In days like these be inspired by all our Prophets and ask the Lord to hear us, remember the Bible says, whosoever believe th... Since I was given the message to write I fear the Lord, that when He gives a message it's not mine to keep but to write it down.

He is the Porter I am the clay. Jesus is the way the Truth and the Life. I cannot explain about my walk in the courtyard but the Holy spirit will take over.

13

IGNITE THE FLAME AND LIGHT THE WORLD

I know that the Lord has shown me a lot of things here on earth, from each town or city I have lived in. He showed me things. Sometimes I prayed not to see if it was too much. I have kept these to myself and few people because it is difficult to share about what others can't see.

Now I feel I can say a few things that I have not been able to share. I feel confident to say after this experience.

Mathew 5:14 says, "You are the Light of the world, a city that is set on a hill and cannot be hidden." On January 1st, 2020 I was awake and had a vision. There was a whip in the sky. It was like light in the shape of a whip.

A voice spoke [My Father's House]. Still in that state, I was taken to a church. I don't know this church, I saw things of darkness, some things looked like black magic things, some things were too dark, I could not look at them.

I understood there is evil in the Churches, I understood they will be shaken like the message that was given to Jeremiah.

Root out and pull down, to destroy and pull down, and then

to build and plant. At the end I saw that a plant was pulled up with its own roots, it was shaken until its roots were a pure white.

All Churches, the Lord said they are the Father's House. Just as I have told a few people I cannot keep it to myself as the Lord is ready for the workmen who are willing to get on the plough and never lookback.

The guideline is His word. All of us should be able to read and get confidence that we are not cheated out of His Kingdom by false information. The Lord wants His Father's house used for the His Glory and for helping souls that are hurting and bring peace to the world, that peace which surpasses all understanding.

For those who are not sure remember if the people die in sin because of not following the Lord's calling, Ezekiel 3:17-18 gives a clear warning because the Lord has made you a watchman of His people. You will be answerable for any of them who are lost in sin.

I have said that before I wrote my first book, I thought it cannot be real that my life story could be a book, but it was not about me, it was about Him in action in a child who was always alone. The Lord was there for me as a child, I knew nothing about Him.

He loves everyone wherever you are. He looks after us, be encouraged. He loves sinners and wants them to come to Him. He wants to comfort lost souls forever and there will be no sadness and no hunger.

Churches have been given to be Shepard for the lost sheep, the Lord is watching. He called the Angels of each Church in the book of Revelation so He could give His thought about the Church and said something about each of those Churches.

The Lord is looking for the Daniels who will pray for the nations. He is looking for the Elijahs who will believe that whatever they ask in His name shall come to pass.

The Lord is looking for people like the Saul of Tarsus, so He can give them a new name, a new tittle and a new job description. Who will find them and show them the way?

The Lord is looking for Prophets like Ezekiel who will call water to run in my well, who will call back to life the hope that was buried. Jesus is looking for the Workmen like Peter where diseases and demons will run from his shadow, because he will understand he has got the key to shut and open the gates of hell without any doubt.

I like the Ezekiel way of prophesy, prophesy against diseases, it's like talking to the diseases to move and instantly shifts. I love this, I would like to do that. Because Jesus said, The Father's will be done here on Earth as it is in Heaven. As he is God in Heaven, He is God here on earth. Let His kingdom come. It is written, Jesus said it, Let Thy Kingdom come.

Proverbs 7:2-4

-keep my commandments and live

-and my law as the apple of your eye

-bind them on your fingers

-write them on the tablet of your heart

- call wisdom your sister and understanding your next of Kin.

Jesus is calling so you can light your light and Light the world. Once on the plough there is no turning back.

Be ready There is no RETREAT.

He says to all of us Follow me.

14

PS; WHAT SHALL I SAY?

I t is almost 8 weeks since I had a walk in the court yard. Still that feeling of saying my Lord knows why remains with me. It was a few days ago as we were praying with my prayer friend Fran, we were reflecting on support we get when we pray through the Holy Spirit. Then she mentioned something about a cloud of witnesses.

We read Hebrews 12:1 and we prayed. I went over chapter 11 and 12 and found something. Though I wrote about Faith and knew the chapter well it became a revelation.

It was just the connection that I thought verse one of Chapter Twelve sounded like the conclusion of chapter 11. Apostle Paul wrote about all these great men of God who reached a goal that God put before them by Faith.

When he comes to something bigger, King David runs short of words and just says [what shall I say] it's too big to put into words. He is an anointed King, what really can you say.

The Apostle indicates to us that they laid a foundation for all that believe, and they are waiting for us to accomplish goals set before us so we can be together with them [In the Courtyard for 144 Thousand].

They, like little fish, went through perils by faith, to give us the word of God and our God will honour our request if we have even little faith. As I was reading Hebrews 11, it was just like the way I walked in the courtyard. It was as if I was walking according to the words of the Apostle. I see these Great men of God as mentioned by the Apostle, I see them, I know them, I know their stories as written by the Apostle, they are walking in the courtyard.

As I walk towards King David's seat, I had to turn a corner and I knew the Glory around Him was going to be too much and I turned again. As I said I was not alone, there was always someone behind me, while I was in heaven. They walked with me.

The Apostle Paul had no words, and I could not go to the Anointed King. I can only think of Ecclesiastes 10: 20,

-do not curse the king

-do not curse the rich

-even in your bedroom

-the bird of the air may hear, they may carry your voice

- a bird in flight may tell the matter.

Maybe the Apostle knew you can't say anything about the King and if it is wrong the word may reach the king.

No secrets better to say nothing than to say something wrong. I so much wanted to pray while I was kneeling down in Heaven, it was very important for me to say the right words in front of God's great people. I was left with no words.

After the verse above was revealed, I was glad I said nothing. The Lord's ways can overcome you and all you can say is beyond words of your mouth. It's true what can you say? Though I knew I was in heaven, I knew I did not belong there. I knew I had to go somewhere, all I wanted was to pray in the Presence of God's people before I left their presence.

That was important to pray while I was in the presence of these great men of God. Also, the words had to be right. They are the Cloud of Witnesses, they have given us testimonies about what our God can do if we have faith like a mustard seed, they are our example, they are ready to cheer us on, to encourage us so they can get that day they are waiting for judgment day.

The Apostle Paul is challenging all of us, they were man like us, they used their faith to do all those recorded miracles.

Our God is the same yesterday and forever, He does not change. Jesus is the way to our salvation there is no other way. I am just full of awe. I have said my songs, dreams and visions, were scriptures but I did not know it for a lifetime its only after writing *The Father's Voice* that the Lord showed me through His ever-present Holy Spirit.

That is what I was trying to explain at the beginning that it is like acting scriptures or role play, I think the Lord is using me to pass a message that He is still communicating with the living and wants to show us the way.

I have no special powers, I am just ordinary and overwhelmed by the Lord's mercies. I now know that I did not get a message because it is already written the Lord used me to highlight the scripture to bring it to light for those that seek Him.

He did it for all the named prophets and He will do it with anyone who answers His call. Whatever the prophets did ask, He is God of Miracles. In days like these, we need miracles not words.

He is the Author, that is why He says [write it down]. Apostle Paul wrote it down clearly and the Lord is reminding His people that, "I am the same yesterday, today and forever. "

Though I was asked to write a book at the beginning, I never thought of a title of the book [Just as I am]. It was just there somehow, I knew the title, I did not think about it.

After its publishing, I saw in the sky. He turned His back and the cloak had the words Just As I Am written. He is still Jesus of Nazareth, the Lamb of God that takes away our sins.

He is coming back to take us so we can be with Him always and we can Sing A New Song with all those that went before us.

What else can I say? He is the Lord, He is the Amen. Like little fish be ready to connect with the Cloud of witnesses and bring back those works which were done before us, the Spirt says, "I am wisdom I am standing on your door way call on me and I will answer."

After my walk in the courtyard, I feel the greatness of the way the Lord prepares us for His work. The gift of faith, like Daniel walking towards the lions' den. I can only repeat my vision walking behind this man, there was no sunlight or moonlight, the light came from Him.

As I walked behind Him everything frightening gave way, because He was in front of me and I was following Him. No evil could harm me. That is [Follow Me].

There is no other way, He leads and we follow Him. He is the way, there is no other way.

Be ready there is no retreat.

15

COMMANDER IN CHIEF

I f you don't hear my voice
How can you know the way
If I have put light in your path
How can you know
If you don't hear my voice?

If you can't hear my voice
Where you are standing?
How can you know I am there?
If I knock at the door
And you don't hear my voice
How can you open the door?

If you don't hear my voice
How can you pray in psalms?
And songs,
If you sing in worship and don't listen to my voice,
How will you sing a new song

I want to give to you?

If you hear my voice
   I will direct your Path.
   I am in your presence always.
   My word is my voice.
   I am your Lord, Hear my voice.

By Commander in Chief

About the Author

Elizabeth Kurangwa is a health professional who is a married mother of 4 and has 7 grandchildren. She is a pleasant person who takes a laid back approach to life but lives well with others and laughs a lot. Being a down to earth person, she has created her boundaries and is not negatively influenced by circumstances around her.

You can connect with me on:
🅵 https://www.facebook.com/mbuya.ot.1

Also by Elizabeth Kurangwa

Just As I AM

https://amzn.to/31xOMK8

This story is about living my life and never looking back because there was nothing exciting in my past. I had an unusual gift of seeing or knowing things that other people did not and living in a superstitious society these are things not usually discussed. I just grew up as I was with no advice about dos and don'ts.

My hope is after reading my story readers will think of other people who are hurting and marginalised without evidence of wrong doing. In these days of advanced science and understanding, my dream is a place where you can go where you will not be judged, where you will be liberated through the word of God. I was blessed to have a pastor who was not bound by superstition. By following my heart, I walked away to a small beautiful Island. This is my story Just As I am.

Elizabeth Kurongwa

The Father's Voice

https://amzn.to/2D7kzZ4

A book that deepens your personal relationship with God.Get inspired and learn the best ways to stay focused on what you need to standout in Life.

Printed in Poland
by Amazon Fulfillment
Poland Sp. z o.o., Wrocław